WORLD BOOK

NORRIE EXPLORES...

BUENOS AIRES

Help Norrie to solve the clues on a fascinating adventure!

World Book, Inc.
180 North LaSalle Street
Suite 900
Chicago, Illinois 60601
USA

For information about other World Book publications, visit our website at www.worldbook.com or call 1-800-WORLDBK (967-5325). For information about sales to schools and libraries, call 1-800-975-3250 (United States), or 1-800-837-5365 (Canada).

Library of Congress Cataloging-in-Publication Data for this volume has been applied for.

Norrie Explores ...
ISBN: 978-0-7166-5303-5 (set, hc.)

Norrie Explores ... Buenos Aires
ISBN: 978-0-7166-5305-9 (hc.)

Also available as:
ISBN: 978-0-7166-5315-8 (e-book)

Printed in India by Thomson Press (India) Limited, Uttar Pradesh, India
1st printing January 2023

Staff

Executive Committee
President: Geoff Broderick
Vice President, Editorial: Tom Evans
Vice President, Finance: Donald D. Keller
Vice President, International: Eddy Kisman
Vice President, Technology: Jason Dole
Director, Human Resources: Bev Ecker

Editorial
Senior Editor/Indexer: Shawn Brennan
Editor/Researcher: Lynn Durbin
Content Creator: Jenna Neely
Curriculum Designer: Caroline Davidson
Project Coordinator: Kaile Kilner
Proofreader: Nathalie Strassheim

Graphics and Design
Senior Visual Communications Designer: Melanie Bender
Senior Media Editor: Rosalia Bledsoe

Acknowledgments

Writer: Izzi Howell
Illustrator: Lizzie Walkley

Developed with World Book by
White-Thomson Publishing LTD
www.wtpub.co.uk

Cover: Norrie artwork by Lizzie Walkley, Advocate Art; © William Silver, Alamy Images

4-7	© Shutterstock
8-9	© William Silver, Alamy Images; © Diego Grandi, Alamy Images
10-11	© ferrantraite/iStock; © DFLC Prints/Shutterstock
12-13	© Cavan Images/Alamy Images; © Nicholas Tinelli, Alamy Images; © Jeffrey Isaac Greenberg 3+/Alamy Images
14-15	© Jeffrey Isaac Greenberg 3+/Alamy Images; © Christian Peters, Alamy Images
16-17	© Ian G Dagnall, Alamy Images; © Hemis/Alamy Images; © gg-foto/Shutterstock
18-19	© Hiroshi Higuchi, Alamy Images; © Carl Dickinson, Alamy Images; © Shutterstock
20-21	© BonnieBC/Shutterstock; © Françoise Emily, Alamy Images; © Panpilai Paipa, Shutterstock
22-23	© Mark Green, Alamy Images; © Jeremy Graham, Alamy Images
24-25	© FluxFactory/iStock; © Aneta Gu, Shutterstock
26-27	© pocholo/Alamy Images
28-29	© Ian Dagnall, Alamy Images; © Alexandr Vorobev, Shutterstock
30-31	© ilyas Ayub, Alamy Images; © pocholo/Alamy Images; © Jeffrey Isaac Greenberg 3+/Alamy Images
32-33	© agefotostock/Alamy Images; © Xiaojun Zhao, Shutterstock
34-35	© DiegoCityExplorer/Shutterstock; © Bernardo Galmarini, Alamy Images
36-37	© Shutterstock
38-39	© Natalia SO, iStock; © saiko3p/Shutterstock
40-41	© Shutterstock
42-43	© kzww/Shutterstock; © Larisa Duka, Shutterstock; © Yadid Levy, Alamy Images; © Ana Carolina Tomas, Shutterstock
46-47	© TLF Images/Shutterstock; Galio (licensed under CC BY-SA 3.0); © Valentina Razumova, Shutterstock; © ampFotoStudio/Shutterstock; © matymonte96/Shutterstock; © mdm7807/Shutterstock; © dsaprin/Shutterstock; © ShinoStock/Shutterstock
48-49	© Armando Oliveira, Shutterstock; © Carolina Jaramillo, Shutterstock; © Lucas Correa Pacheco, Shutterstock; © Maria Elisa Rol, Shutterstock; © Gary Yim, Shutterstock; Eduardo Lacerda (licensed under CC BY 2.0)
50-51	© Shutterstock

— Contents —

Help me solve the clues on my journey through Buenos Aires!

Whew! It's quite an adventure!

Welcome to Buenos Aires!

Hi, I'm Norrie! I'm a puffin. I love to travel the world and explore different cities around the globe.

Today, I'm in Buenos Aires, the capital city of Argentina. Argentina is a country on the continent of South America. Have you ever visited Buenos Aires or Argentina before? Buenos Aires is a port city. It was founded in the 1500's by Spanish colonizers. Today, Argentina is an independent country, but people still speak Spanish. In fact, Buenos Aires means *fair winds* in Spanish! It is one of the largest cities in South America by population, with over 15 million inhabitants.

Behind this beautiful fountain and monument is the National Congress – an important government building.

My Argentinian friend Maria sent me a letter with lots of suggestions and photos of things to do and see in Buenos Aires. She lives here for part of the year, but isn't here at the moment, as she has migrated north for some warmer weather! Unfortunately I just dropped Maria's letter in the fountain and now it's a bit hard to read!

Will you help me piece together the parts of her letter and find my way around the city?

Plaza de Mayo

Mayo must be from Plaza de Mayo! This is a large square in the oldest part of Buenos Aires.

Plaza de Mayo is named for the protest that led to Argentina's independence from Spain. Hundreds of years ago, the Spanish Empire controlled lands all over North and South America, including Argentina. In May of 1810, Argentinians gathered in this spot to protest Spanish rule. (Mayo is Spanish for May.) Since then, there have been many protests and celebrations here. Today this beautiful space looks much like it did when it was redesigned in 1884.

There are lots of interesting buildings around the square. Over there is the Cabildo, the old town hall. It's the only building left over from when Argentina was a Spanish colony. Now it is a museum. And there on the corner of the plaza is a church called the Catedral Metropolitana. Soon after Argentina gained its independence, Buenos Aires began to grow. Plaza de Mayo was the center. The rest of the city built up around it.

This is the second town hall that has stood on this spot. The original town hall, which was built in 1580, was made from adobe (dried earth) and straw. The building that stands today was built in the 1700's.

Casa Rosada

As soon as I saw the pink, I knew it had to be the Casa Rosada!

This huge pink building is where the president of Argentina works. Some people call it the Pink House or Government House. Up until the 1800's, there was a Spanish fort here. It was torn down to build a customs house (a government building where people kept track of items that came into and out of the country). This building was later chosen as the center of government and painted pink. It has kept its famous pink color ever since!

No one is really sure why the building was originally painted pink. Some people think it was to make opposing political parties happy. One party's color was red and the other's was white, so pink was a good compromise! Other people believe that the building was once painted with cow's blood as paint peeled away in the warm, damp weather. Yuck! Today, the pink walls of the Casa Rosada bring lots of fun color to Plaza de Mayo.

There are many halls, patios, and reception rooms inside the Casa Rosada, as well as a museum.

Avenida 9 de Julio

If you're looking for wide, look no farther!

Avenida 9 (Nueve) de Julio isn't just the widest street in Buenos Aires, it's the widest avenue in the world! The 1.9-mile (3-kilometer) street takes up an entire city block with its 16 lanes of traffic. Every intersection on Avenida 9 de Julio has a set of traffic lights, so it can take a while for pedestrians to cross from one side to the other. The name 9 de Julio means July 9th in English. July 9th is Argentina's Independence Day.

The white, pointy monument in the middle of the avenue is called an obelisk. It was built to honor the 400th anniversary of the city's founding. Think of it as a huge birthday cake candle!

It marks the date that the country became independent from Spain. Do you have any places named after important dates where you live?

The construction of this street started all the way back in the 1930's. It wasn't finished until 1980! The avenue was modeled on the Champs Élysées, a famous avenue in Paris, France. Four of the lanes were turned into bus-only lanes in 2014 to reduce the number of cars on the road. One of Buenos Aires's underground lines also runs under the avenue.

Centro Cultural Kirchner

You don't need a guidebook to identify the CCK (Centro Cultural Kirchner). Its name is written right across the front! This is the city's cultural center, a place where people come to enjoy the arts. The building is very big and grand. It takes up the entire block! Thousands of people come here every day for free classes, concerts, and exhibits.

The CCK opened in 2015, but the building it's in has been here for a long time. When it opened back in 1928, it was the biggest building in all of Argentina. Maria's notes don't say what it was before, though. Let's hunt for clues to help jog my memory.

Look – I see mailboxes on the wall over there. And these long marble counters seem like good places to write a letter. Oh, it seems that this building used to be the city's central post office!

The CCK's main concert hall is called La Sala Sinfonica, which means symphonic hall in English. It's like a big metal balloon on stilts. The design makes the sound inside just right. It's big enough to hold an audience of 1,950 people.

Puerto Madero

I've got it! This riverside neighborhood is called Puerto Madero and it's the perfect place for a stroll.

It used to be part of the main port in Buenos Aires, but wasn't used much after 1926. In the 1990's, lots of old warehouses around here were turned into restaurants, offices, and apartments. Today, it's one of the most popular parts of the city. Lots of people come to Puerto Madero to eat, walk along the river, and visit cinemas, theaters and galleries.

This bridge is called "Puente de la Mujer" or the Woman's Bridge. A section of the bridge can rotate 90 degrees to let boats pass through.

The water that flows through Puerto Madero is part of the Río de la Plata. This is a large estuary where two South American rivers, the Uruguay and Paraná, join together and flow into the Atlantic Ocean. Buenos Aires is built on the western shore of the Río de la Plata.

After Argentina became independent from Spain, its people could trade freely with the nations of Europe. The port on the Río de la Plata became very busy, and Argentina became a wealthy nation. Buenos Aires was such an important port that its people became known as porteños. That means people of the port in Spanish.

San Telmo

Buenos Aires has many different barrios (neighborhoods). The oldest barrio is San Telmo – S and T, just like in Maria's notes!

For hundreds of years, almost everyone in the city lived here in San Telmo. But deadly diseases called cholera and yellow fever started to spread in the late 1800's. People wanted to get away from the crowded conditions, which helped to spread disease. Families who could afford it moved north.

The houses they left behind were turned into apartment buildings. Many of the immigrants pouring into Buenos Aires found a place to live here. I can tell that San Telmo is old because the streets are narrow and paved with round stones. In other barrios, the streets are wide, with modern pavement.

San Telmo doesn't just have old streets and buildings. It's also a great place to shop for antiques! There are lots of antique shops and even an outdoor antique and craft fair once a week in Plaza Dorrego, which stretches 13 blocks to Plaza de Mayo.

When the craft and antiques fair isn't on, Plaza Dorrego is filled with tables from cafes and bars. What a great spot for a snack!

La Boca

The neighborhood of La Boca is well known for its brightly painted houses.

The most famous street in La Boca is called El Caminito. That means little street in Spanish. The street is a museum in the open air. As you walk along, you can look up at the paintings and sculptures.

Before there was art here, people used this area as a dump, filling it with trash! Before that, it was covered in railroad tracks. And before that, there was just a small stream with a little bridge. I think I like the way it is now the best.

El Caminito became famous because of a song called "Caminito." It was composed by Juan de Dios Filiberto. It's actually a tango song. The tango is a kind of music and dance invented by the porteños. There are many places in La Boca where people come together to dance the tango. Let's see if I can find one.

What a colorful restaurant! Many Italian immigrants settled in this neighborhood, so many restaurants sell traditional Italian dishes, such as pizza.

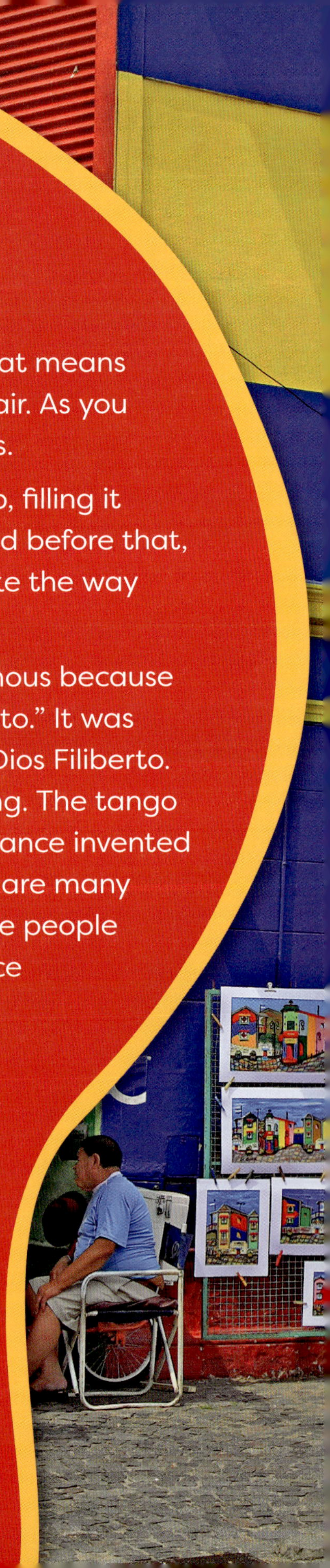

Don't forget to look up when you're on El Caminito. Some of the sculptures are on the balconies of the colorful houses.
Look! What is that couple doing?
CENTRO de EXPOSICIONES
CAMINITO
TANGO
BAR-CAFE
ARTE
FREE ENTRY
DEPORTES
T-SHIRTS

Tango

La Boca is also an excellent spot to watch couples dancing the tango.

This famous dance started right here in Buenos Aires in the 1880's. It later spread around the world. Today, it is a popular dance in many countries, but Buenos Aires is still its home, so I had to check it out for myself!

Today, there are many styles of tango dance, including the original Argentinian tango, new modern tango, and ballroom tango, which is used in ballroom competitions.

The tango is famous for its sharp kicks, strong emotions, and the way the dancers hold their arms. It is influenced by various dances from Africa, South America and Europe. Different communities of immigrants to Argentina came together and combined their own traditional dances to create something new and original.

You can see people dancing tango in many different places in Buenos Aires – on the street, in bars and in special tango shows. There are even massive tango festivals where tango fans from around the world come together to share their love for the dance.

Tango music is usually played on the guitar, or by a small band made up of violins, accordions, piano and double bass. Sometimes a singer joins in as well!

La Bombonera

This giant football stadium is located in La Boca. (Football is known as soccer in the United States.)

Its real name is Estadio Alberto J. Armando, but everyone calls it La Bombonera, which means chocolate box in English. Some say the stadium looks like a giant chocolate box. It is painted in the team colors, yellow and blue.

The team that plays here is called the Boca Juniors, but that doesn't mean kids play here. Argentinians love football, and this men's team is one of the most successful teams in the country. Many of its players have played for the Argentinian national team in such competitions as the World Cup. You can learn more about the team and its players at a museum inside the stadium.

As well as football matches, the stadium also hosts concerts. Famous singers come from around the world to perform their hits. The unusual "D" shape of the stadium means that everyone in the audience can hear the performance very well.

There are enough seats and standing room for 54,000 people to attend a match at La Bombonera. Would you rather stand up or sit down?

Mate

Puff! I need a break after all that exploring.

And I think I've worked out what Maria was recommending – a traditional drink called mate, which is very popular in Argentina. It's made by pouring hot water on the dried leaves of the yerba mate plant. It's a bit like making tea, but it's prepared in a special way.

You also need the right equipment: a special cup (also called a mate) and a metal straw. The cup is actually made from a dried gourd. A gourd is a bit like a type of pumpkin that can be dried out and used as a container. The metal straw has a filter on the end so that you don't suck up the mate leaves as well as the drink! That wouldn't taste so good.

Porteños come together to drink mate with their friends and family. Everyone shares the same cup and straw. More water is added to the leaves to make enough for everyone! Like tea and coffee, mate contains caffeine. So now I have lots of energy to carry on exploring Buenos Aires. Where will Maria's notes take me next?

This is all you need to enjoy a drink of mate. Just add hot water!

Teatro Colón

If you want to watch opera in Buenos Aires, you have to visit the Teatro Colón.

This big building is one of the world's best opera houses. Opera is a kind of play in which people sing to music as well as speak, instead of speaking only. Let's peek inside!

The Teatro Colón started in 1857 but closed to build the current building in 1888. The theater reopened in 1908. I love the pink marble staircases in the lobby. There are lots of other special details in the building, like stained glass and a chandelier (fancy light fixture) with 735 bulbs.

The main theater is huge! There are more than 2,400 soft red seats for the audience, plus room for people to stand in the galleries higher up. The theater was built so that it's easy to hear the performers from anywhere in it. The singers don't even use microphones. The famous opera singer Luciano Pavarotti complained that the sound quality here was so good that people could hear every mistake!

A lot of things happen behind the scenes. Hundreds of people work in the building's big basement to make costumes, build sets, and do the performers' hair and makeup. It's like an underground city down there! After the show, I'm going on a tour to see it for myself.

.... Florida
for shopping
Hmmm, what could Maria mean by that?

Calle Florida

After sitting down to watch the opera, it's nice to stretch my legs a bit.

Calle Florida is a good place to walk because the street is for pedestrians only – it is closed to traffic. There are also a lot of shops here. Maybe I'll find some souvenirs!

One of the best places to shop on Calle Florida is a shopping mall called Galerías Pacífico. When the building opened in 1889, it was the National Museum of Fine Arts. (The museum is in another barrio now.) There are still paintings here, though. Look up! Argentine artists painted 12 scenes on the cupola (domed ceiling).

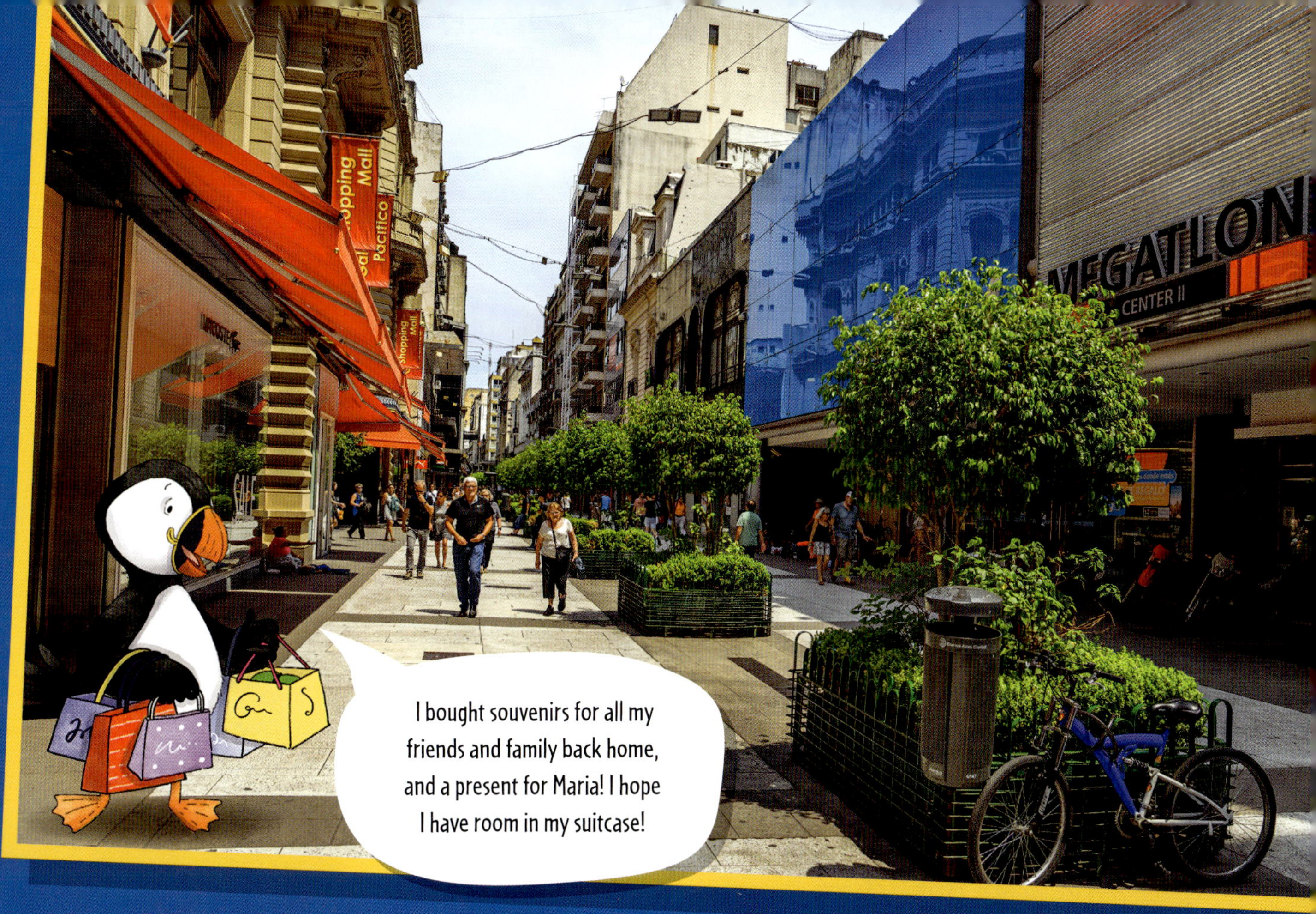

I'm going to head back out onto Calle Florida to do some people watching. I see a lot of people with shopping bags. (Porteños love to shop.) I see street performers who are singing or playing the guitar. I see workers in kioskos, little stands where they sell newspapers and candy. I see a lot of people in business suits who seem to be in a hurry. This is because there are a lot of banks and offices nearby.

Basílica del Santísimo Sacramento

Those three towers belong to the Basílica del Santísimo Sacramento – a beautiful Catholic church.

It actually has five towers, but you can only see three from the front.

Most people in Argentina are of the Roman Catholic faith, so Buenos Aires has a lot of Catholic churches. The outsides of some of these churches look very plain, but others are quite fancy. The Basílica del Santísimo Sacramento looks fancy from the outside *and* the inside, so it's well worth a visit! It has beautiful stained glass windows and the floor is a mosaic. This means that it is covered in many tiny colored tiles that form pictures and designs.

The Basílica del Santísimo Sacramento isn't the main Catholic church in Buenos Aires. The most important church here is the Catedral Metropolitana, which is located on the Plaza de Mayo. The body of Argentina's most famous hero is buried here. His name was General José de San Martín. In the early 1800's, he fought to help Argentina gain independence from Spain.

Kavanagh Building

Here I am, looking up at the Kavanagh Building, one of the most important landmarks in Buenos Aires.

This skyscraper was the tallest building in South America when it opened in 1936. It must have been very exciting to watch the building grow taller and taller by the day!

Inside the Kavanagh Building are 105 apartments. When it opened, the apartments were considered very luxurious because they contained the most exciting modern technology of the 1930's, such as air conditioning, elevators and telephone connections! Today, these things come as standard, but at that time, they would only have been found in rich people's homes. Today, the apartments are still very expensive. Wouldn't it be an amazing place to live!

Today, there are many more skyscrapers in Buenos Aires. Many of them are located in Puerto Madero, which I visited earlier today! The tallest is the Alvear Tower, which measures 771 feet (235 meters) high. It's actually the tallest building in the whole of Argentina! Like the Kavanagh Building, it also has apartments inside.

Floralis Genérica

Wow! That's a big flower! This massive metal sculpture, named Floralis Genérica, sits in a pool of water in a square next to the National Museum of Fine Arts.

It was built in 2002 and has been a popular landmark for tourists and porteños ever since. I'm so glad Maria included it in her notes!

Floralis Genérica looks pretty impressive right now, but if you visit the sculpture at 8 a.m. or at sunset, you're in for an exciting show. The flower opens its petals every morning, and closes them again in the evening, just like some real flowers do. The whole process takes about 20 minutes.

The sculpture's stainless steel petals reflect the buildings and plaza around it.

The petals stay closed in windy weather, but stay open all day on special national holidays.

When the petals are closed, the statue measures 85 feet (26 meters) wide. When its petals are fully open, it measures a massive 105 feet (32 meters) across. That's got to be one of the biggest flowers on Earth!

After the petals have closed for the night, the flower glows red.

El Cementerio de la Recoleta

I know what you're thinking. A cemetery is a graveyard, which may seem a little scary. Please don't worry!

The Recoleta Cemetery, or El Cementerio de la Recoleta as it's called in Spanish, is a very beautiful place. It's a bit like a small, quiet city. There's no grass, like you'd see in many graveyards. Instead you can stroll down sidewalks.

These small buildings hold the bodies of the dead. There are many shapes and sizes. Some are decorated with statues of marble or stone. Each mausoleum seems to look different, doesn't it?

This was the first public cemetery in Buenos Aires. It opened in 1822. Getting a spot here isn't easy! It costs a lot of money. But some of the graves are so old that they have been forgotten. That's why some of the mausoleums seem so nice and new, and others are dusty and crumbling.

Presidents, war heroes, celebrities, and scientists are all buried in this cemetery.

About 75 stray cats live in the Recoleta Cemetery. Volunteers feed the graveyard cats twice a day and make sure they are in good health.

Parque Tres de Febrero

If you're looking for roses in Buenos Aires, you have to stop by Parque Tres de Febrero to see the famous rose garden, the Rosedal de Palermo.

Parque Tres de Febrero, also called Palermo Woods, is the largest park in the city. The Rosedal de Palermo contains thousands and thousands of roses – too many to count.

Tres de Febrero means February 3rd in Spanish. On this day in 1852, a dictator (harsh ruler) was overthrown, and some of his land was turned into this park.

As well as the rose garden, there are also lakes, woods, and a Japanese-style garden. People come here to walk, go jogging, have a picnic, or take a boat ride on the lake. What should I do first?

Up ahead is a big building that's round like a ball. That's the Planetario Galileo Galilei, a planetarium named after a famous Italian scientist of the 1600's. A planetarium is a place where you learn about the planets and the stars.

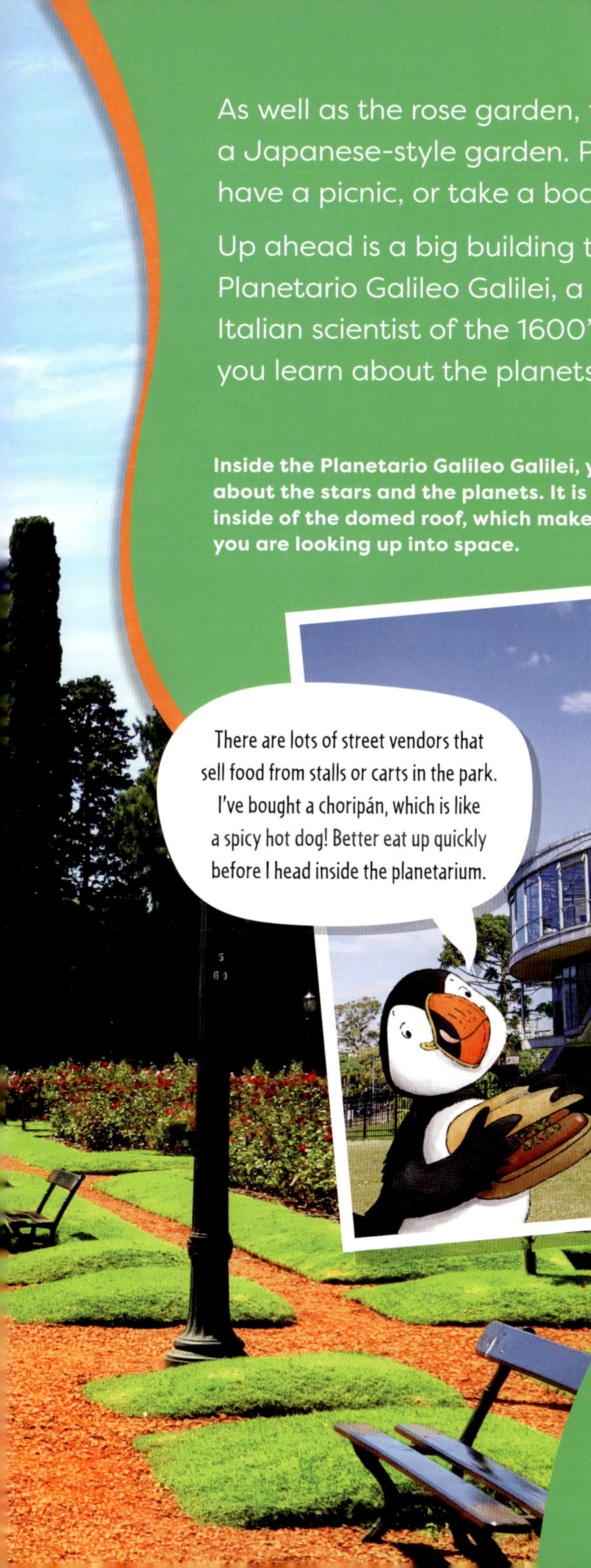

Inside the Planetario Galileo Galilei, you can watch a show about the stars and the planets. It is projected on the inside of the domed roof, which makes it feel like you are looking up into space.

Pampas

To make the most of my new hat, I've come out to the pampas, the wide grassy plains that lie just outside the city.

The land here is very flat and very grassy. The pampas cover a big chunk of Argentina – nearly one-third! The soil here is fertile, which is good for farming and ranching.

And ranching is just why I'm here! I'm here to visit an estancia. That's Spanish for cattle ranch. Hundreds and hundreds of years ago, there were no cattle in Argentina. The animals arrived with Spanish explorers in the 1500's. Can you guess what happened next? Cattle loved grazing on all this flat, grassy land. They roamed and spread across the pampas. Today, there are more cows than people in Argentina.

The pampas are home to cowboys called gauchos. That brings me back to my hat! It's a traditional gaucho boina – a type of flat hat, like a beret. Many gauchos have a mix of European and Indigenous (native) ancestry.

The pampas are also home to many wild animals, such as this pampas fox. If you're lucky, you might spot a rhea, which is like a South American ostrich, or a guanaco, a relative of the llama.

At first, gauchos caught wild cattle and sold them for leather, not meat. Over time, though, meat became more important than leather. Most gauchos started working for estancias instead of by themselves.

Dinner at the parilla

Talk about perfect timing!

Maria's recommendations have led me to a parilla restaurant just as my stomach was starting to rumble. A parilla is a steakhouse. The steak comes from the cattle that we saw roaming the pampas. In Buenos Aires, there are many different parillas to choose from. I know it seems late, but this is early for dinner in Buenos Aires. Most porteños won't start their evening meal until 9:00 or 10:00 p.m.

Let's take a look at the menu. I think I'm going to order carne (beef). Asado is steak cooked over an open fire. You can dip each bite in chimichurri, a tasty sauce made with olive oil, garlic, and parsley.

Time for dessert now! Dulce de leche is very popular here in Argentina. It's a sweet sauce that tastes like caramel. You could get it drizzled over a custard called flan, or baked into cakes and pastries. But I have a better idea. Let's go for gelato, a thick, smooth Italian-style ice cream. Gelato is easy to find in a city that has welcomed so many Italian immigrants.

These tasty cookies filled with dulce de leche are called alfajores.

BUENOS AIRES
- MAP -

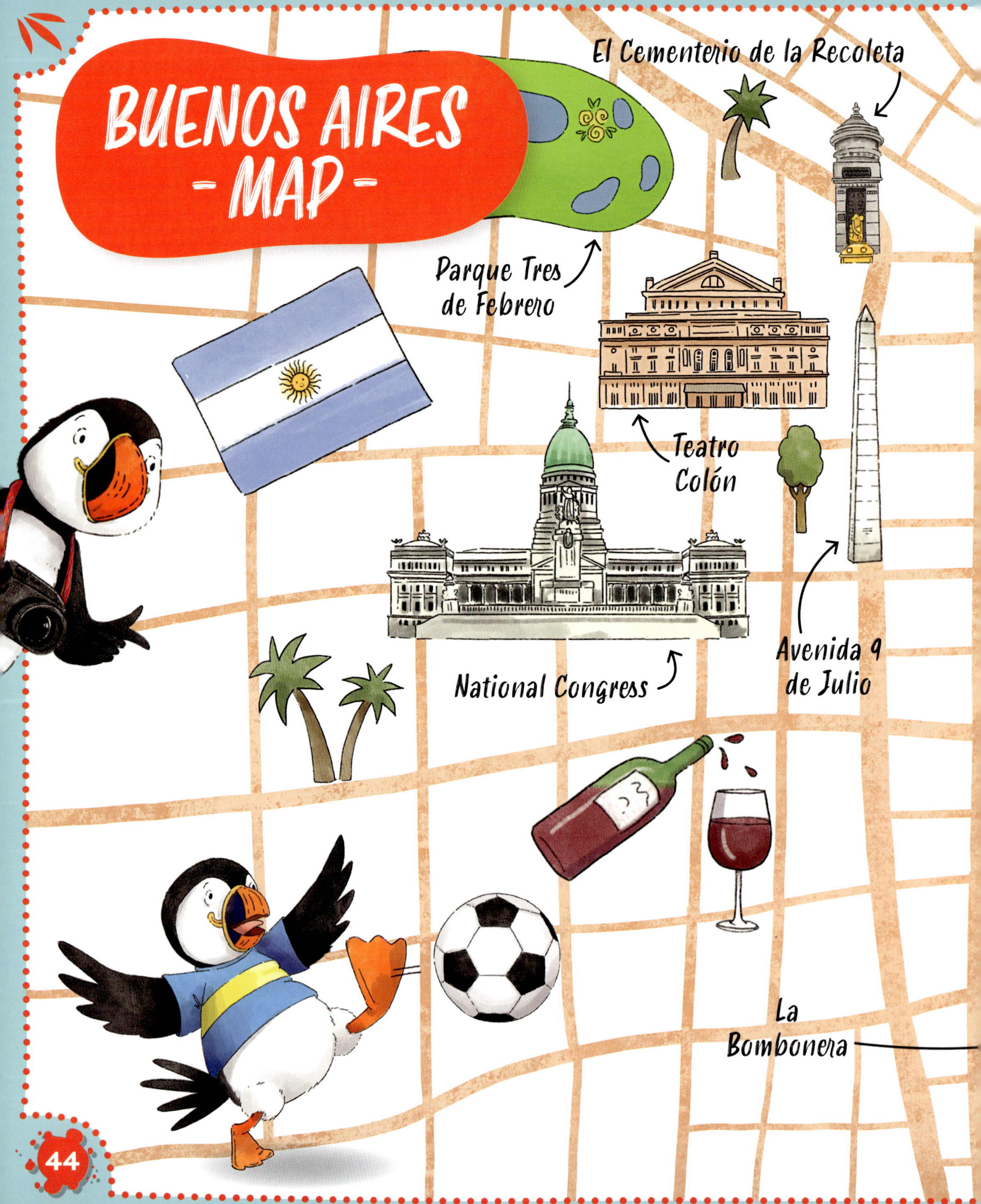

Floralis Genérica
Kavanagh Building
Basílica del Santísimo Sacramento
Río de la Plata
Centro Cultural Kirchner
Alvear Tower
Calle Florida
Plaza de Mayo
Puente de la Mujer
Puerto Madero
Casa Rosada
San Telmo
La Boca
El Caminito

A Day in Buenos Aires

Start at the Museum of Latin American Art of Buenos Aires, or Malba for short. This museum is on a mission to collect, conserve, study, and create awareness of Latin American art from the early 20th century through today.

Pick up a souvenir book in Spanish at what has been described as the world's most beautiful bookstore, El Ateno Grand Splendid!

You must be getting hungry! Stop at a local restaurant for some empanadas and arroz con leche!

Empanadas are a type of baked or fried turnover consisting of pastry and filling.

Arroz con leche is a kind of rice pudding.

Load up your SUBE travel card and use it to take public transportation like the bus or subte (underground train) to the opera house!

Catch a show or just enjoy the ornate beauty that is Teatro Colón!

Take a tour of the underground offices and workshops for some behind-the-scenes magic!

Cross the famous Woman's Bridge to the Puerto Madero District, where the restaurant industry has boomed, for some dinner.

Burn off that evening meal with some fun Buenos Aires night life! Will you be caught doing the tango on the dance floor?

Where Am I?

Destination 1

This popular tourist attraction was built in 2002.

At its largest, this massive, metal sculpture can reach 105 feet (32 meters) across!

The flower's stainless steel petals beautifully reflect the surrounding city.

Destination 2

The president of Argentina works here.

Before becoming the Government House, this building was a customs house and the location of a Spanish fort.

No one knows for sure why this building was originally painted pink.

Destination 3

Look at all the beautiful mausoleums as you stroll down the sidewalks of this "small city."

As you walk, see if you can spot any of the 75 cats who call this place home.

This cemetery first opened over 200 years ago!

Destination 4

This flat, grassy land is located just outside the city and covers about one third of all of Argentina!

Gauchos raise cattle out here, often to be sold for meat.

You may be able to spot wild animals such as certain species of foxes or even rheas here!

Destination 5

This is known as the oldest barrio in all of Buenos Aires.

Cholera and yellow fever spread through this neighborhood during the late 1800's.

Today, this is a great destination for antique shopping and admiring the old architecture.

Destination 6

This place got its nickname because people think it looks like a chocolate box!

More than 50,000 fans can attend concerts and football matches here.

This stadium is home to the Boca Juniors, one of the most successful football teams in Argentina.

Answers on page 55

Photos from Buenos Aires

Centro Cultural Kirchner

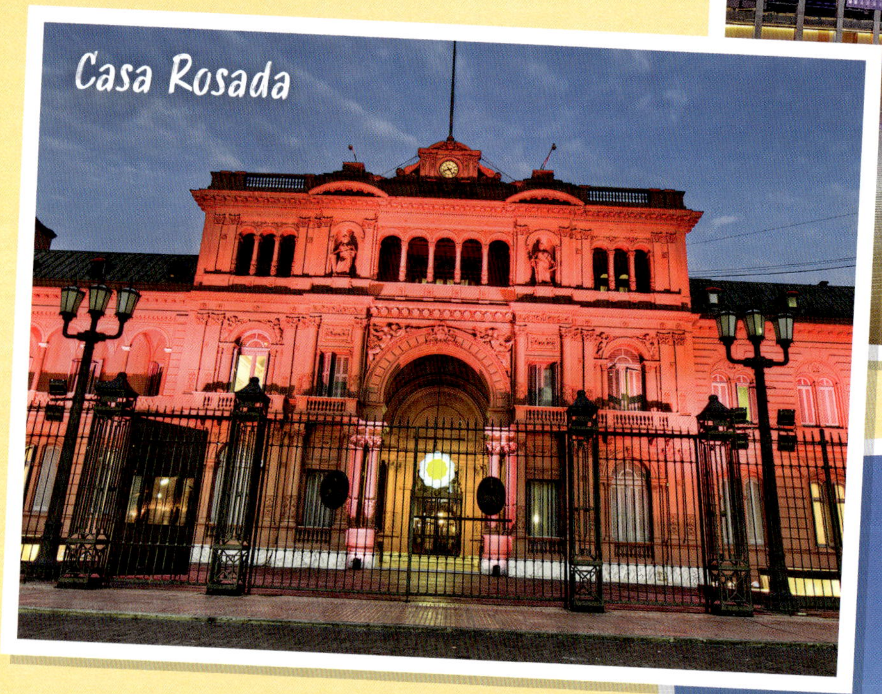

Casa Rosada

Puerto Madero

Teatro Colón

Avenida 9 de Julio

Parque Tres de Febrero

La Boca

Engage Your Reader

Activate background knowledge, set the purpose for reading, and monitor comprehension with this tried-and-true reading strategy!

Work with your reader(s) to create a KWL chart. Take some time to discuss what students already KNOW about Buenos Aires as well as what they WONDER about the city. You will revisit what they LEARNED after reading the book.

KNOW	WONDER	LEARNED

1. Have readers preview the structure of this text by flipping through the pages. Page 5 describes how clues are included for Norrie the puffin's next destinations.
2. Set the tone for reading: *As you read, think about all the different places in Buenos Aires and how history, culture, and people have shaped them into what they are today.*
3. After reading each section, revisit the KWL chart. Brainstorm what readers LEARNED from this section and add it to the chart. Your reader can add other wonderings they may have had, too!

Consider these questions to guide the brainstorming process:

- Why is location important to places, history, and culture?
- What patterns do you notice in the placement of things around the city of Buenos Aires?
- What makes Buenos Aires unique?

Use these comprehension questions to help your reader(s) check their understanding as they navigate the text.

p. 6-7 Why is Plaza de Mayo an important part of Buenos Aires?

p. 8-9 What is the Pink House?

p. 10-11 What makes Avenida 9 de Julio unique?

How did this famous location get its name?

p. 12-13 How has the Centro Cultural Kirchner (CCK) building changed over time?

What happens at the CCK today?

p. 14-15 What do people like to do in the Puerto Madero neighborhood?

p. 16-17 For what is the San Telmo neighborhood best known? What evidence in the text supports your answer?

p. 18-19 How did the La Boca neighborhood become famous for tango?

p. 20-21 What makes tango dancing unique?

p. 22-23 Why is La Bombonera a great stadium for football and concerts alike?

p. 24-25 What is mate and how do people drink it?

p. 26-27 Why did Luciano Pavarotti, a famous opera singer, complain about the Teatro Colón architecture? What does that tell you about its design?

p. 28-29 What would you enjoy most about Calle Florida? Why?

p. 30-31 What is special about the design of the Basílica del Santísimo Sacramento, especially compared to other churches in Buenos Aires?

p. 32-33 Why might the Kavanagh Building be considered one of the most important landmarks in Buenos Aires?

What is the tallest building in Argentina today?

p. 34-35 What happens at the Floralis Genérica statue every morning at 8 a.m. and every evening at sunset?

p. 36-37 What is a mausoleum?

Make an inference: Why might volunteers feed the 75 stray cats that live in this cemetery?

p. 38-39 If you took a trip to Parque Tres de Febrero, what would you most like to do and why?

p. 40-41 What are the pampas and where are they located?

Who are gauchos and what do they do on the pampas?

p. 42-43 Describe the dinner Norrie the puffin had at the parilla.

What food would you most like to try? Why?

Extend Through Writing

Norrie the puffin just took you on a tour of Buenos Aires, Argentina! Based on the places highlighted in this book, where would you like to visit in Buenos Aires?

Your written response should include:

- An introduction, including a general statement about Buenos Aires
- At least three places you would like to visit and at least three reasons why these places interest you
- A conclusion in which you briefly restate your interest in these three famous Buenos Aires destinations

Copy this graphic organizer onto another sheet of paper or visit **www.worldbook.com/resources** to download and print a copy. Use it to help you plan your writing.

Introduction:		
Destination 1	Destination 2	Destination 3
Reason 1	Reason 1	Reason 1
Reason 2	Reason 2	Reason 2
Reason 3	Reason 3	Reason 3
Conclusion:		

Answers

Where Am I? answers, p. 48-49:

1. Floralis Genérica, 2. Casa Rosada, 3. El Cementerio de la Recoleta, 4. Pampas, 5. San Telmo neighborhood, 6. La Bombonera

Comprehension question answers, p. 53:

p. 6-7

Plaza de Mayo is an important part of Buenos Aires because it marks the spot where Argentinians gathered in 1810 to protest Spanish rule.

p. 8-9

The Pink House, also called Casa Rosada, is where the president of Argentina lives and works. Because of this, some people also call it the Government House.

p. 10-11

Avenida 9 de Julio is unique because it is the widest avenue in the world, measuring 1.9 miles, or 3 kilometers! The street's name translates to July 9th in English and is named after Argentina's Independence Day.

p. 12-13

The CCK building opened in 1928 as the city's central post office. Today it is a popular cultural center where people gather to celebrate and enjoy the arts.

p. 14-15

The Puerto Madero neighborhood is located next to a beautiful riverside. People enjoy walking around the area, eating at nice restaurants, and visiting cinemas, theaters, and galleries.

p. 16-17

The San Telmo neighborhood is known for being the oldest barrio in Buenos Aires! Its narrow streets paved with round stones remind visitors of its history.

p. 18-19

The La Boca neighborhood is well known for El Caminito street, which became famous in large part because of a popular tango song called Caminito.

p. 20-21

Tango is a unique style of dance that is famous for sharp kicks, strong emotions, and carefully held arms. There are many styles of tango dancing, but all are influenced by dances from Africa, South America, and Europe.

p. 22-23

La Bombonera is a famous stadium in the La Boca barrio. Its unusual D shape allows the fans at football matches and concerts alike to hear and see very well.

p. 24-25

Mate is a traditional Argentinian drink. To make mate, pour hot water over dried yerba leaves and drink it using a special cup and straw.

p. 26-27

The famous opera singer Luciano Pavarotti once complained that the Teatro Colón had such good sound quality, the audience could hear his every mistake! That tells us the opera house was well designed and constructed.

p. 28-29

Answers may vary.

p. 30-31

The Basílica del Santísimo Sacramento is well known for being a beautiful Catholic church. Whereas most Catholic churches in Buenos Aires are plain on the outside, this one is ornate both inside and out.

p. 32-33

The Kavanagh Building might be considered one of the most important landmarks in Buenos Aires because it was the tallest building in all of South America when it opened in 1936. Today, the tallest Argentinian building is Alvear Tower, which measures 771 feet (235 meters) tall.

p. 34-35

Every morning at 8 a.m. the Floralis Genérica's metal petals open. Just like real flowers, the petals close up again at sunset each night.

p. 36-37

A mausoleum is a small building that holds the bodies of the dead, as opposed to burying them in the ground.

Cemetery volunteers likely continue to feed the 75-some stray cats that live here so they continue to protect the grounds from mice and other rodents.

p. 38-39

Answers may vary.

p. 40-41

The pampas are the wide, grassy plains found just outside of Buenos Aires. Gauchos, or cowboys, live and work on cattle ranches here.

p. 42-43

Norrie the puffin had asado, chimichurri, dulce de leche, and gelato for dinner at the parilla! Answers may vary about which food readers would enjoy most and why.

Glossary

barrio *(BAHR ree oh)* Neighborhood

estuary *(EHS choo ehr ee)* A coastal river valley flooded by an ocean. Most estuaries are shaped like funnels, with the wide end toward the sea.

pedestrian *(puh DEHS tree uhn)* A person who goes on foot; for or used by pedestrians.

porteño *(pohr TAYN yoh)* A person who lives in Buenos Aires

tango *(TANG goh)* The tango is a ballroom dance for a couple in slow 2/4 or 4/4 time. The dancers mix long, slow steps with short, quick steps, sometimes making sudden turns and striking dramatic poses.

Index